DISCOVERING PSYCHOLOGY

Nina Crosby ~ Elizabeth Marten

D.O.K. Publishers, Inc., Buffalo, NY 14214

UNIQUELY YOURS:

The purchase of this book entitles the buyer to exclusive reproduction rights of the Student Activity Pages. Permission to reproduce these pages is extended to the purchaser only. No other part of this publication may be reproduced, stored in a retrieval system, or transmitted in any form or by any means, electronic, mechanical photocopying, recording, or otherwise, without prior written permission of the D.O.K. Publishers, Inc., 71 Radcliffe Rd., Buffalo, NY 14214.

Illustrations by Susan Kondziela

ISBN 0-914634-94-1

©1981
D.O.K. Publishers, Inc.
Buffalo, NY 14214

CONTENTS

Major Categories in the Affective Domain Krathwohl's Taxonomy		2
To the Teacher		4
I	Psychology in Perspective	6
II	Characteristics of Behavior	11
III	Learning	18
IV	Motivation	26
V	Emotions	32
VI	Thought and Problem Solving	38
VII	Personality	43
VIII	Relationships	50
IX	Careers Related to Human Behavior	55
X	An Image of Me	58
XI	Student Pages	62

MAJOR CATEGORIES IN THE AFFECTIVE DOMAIN OF THE TAXONOMY
OF EDUCATIONAL OBJECTIVES (KRATHWOHL, 1964)

Categories	Behaviors	Action Words
Receiving -- Student willingness to attend to particular phenomena or stimuli. The teacher is concerned with getting, holding, and directing the students' attention.	Attentive listening Awareness of importance of learning Sensitive to human needs/social problems Accepting of racial/cultural differences Attends closely to activities of the classroom	Asks, chooses, describes, follows, gives, holds, identifies, locates, names, points to, selects, sits erect, relies, uses
Responding -- Active participation on the part of the student. Learning outcomes emphasize acquiescence in responding, willingness to respond, or satisfaction in responding.	Completes homework Obeys rules Participates in discussion Volunteers for special tasks Shows interest in subject Enjoys helping others	Answers, assists, compiles, conforms, discusses, greets, helps, labels, performs, practices, presents, reads, recites, reports, selects, tells, writes
Valuing -- The worth or value a student attaches to a particular object, phenomenon, or behavior. Based on internalization and a set of specified values. "Attitudes" and "appreciation" would fall into this category.	Demonstrates belief in democratic process Appreciates good literature/art/music Appreciates application of study to everyday life Shows concern for welfare of others Demonstrates problem-solving attitude Committed to social improvement	Completes, describes, differentiates, explains, follows, forms, initiates, invites, joins, justifies, proposes, reads, reports, selects, shares, studies, works

MAJOR CATEGORIES IN THE AFFECTIVE DOMAIN OF THE TAXONOMY

OF EDUCATIONAL OBJECTIVES (KRATHWOHL, 1964)

Categories	Behaviors	Action Words
Organization -- Concerned with bringing together different values, resolving conflicts, and beginning to build an internally consistent value system. Emphasis is on comparing, relating, and synthesizing values. Conceptualization of a value and the organization of a value system would fall into this category.	Recognizes need for balance between freedom/responsibility Appreciates systematic planning in problem-solving Accepts responsibility for own behavior Understands and accepts own strengths/limitations Formulates a life plan in harmony with own abilities, interests and beliefs	Adheres, alters, arranges, combines, compares, completes, defends, explains, generalizes, identifies, integrates, modifies, orders, organizes, prepares, relates, synthesizes
Characterization By a Value or Value Complex -- The individual has a value system that has controlled his behavior for a sufficiently long time for him to have developed a characteristic "life style". Major emphasis is on the fact that the behavior is typical or characteristic of the individual.	Displays safety consciousness Demonstrates self-reliance in working independently Practices cooperation in group activities Uses objective approach in problem-solving Demonstrates industry/punctuality/self-discipline Maintains good health habits	Acts, discriminates, displays, influences, listens, modifies, performs, practices, proposes, qualifies, questions, revises, serves, solves, uses, verifies

TO THE TEACHER

Students are often very concerned with the problems of everyday living and with their places in society. Discovering Psychology structures activities designed to examine difficult and important questions relative to life and life's problems. Historical perspective is developed to build an understanding of the field as a science. Then students move into a variety of explorations that deal with their personal behaviors, reactions, and inter-actions with others.

Discovering Psychology is a developmental approach to the examination of self and personal relationships to society.

Discovering Psychology helps students:

- --- Understand the field of psychology and its importance to man.
- --- Become more in tune with their personal feelings and behaviors.
- --- Become more sensitive to the differences among people.
- --- Become logical thinkers.
- --- Apply skills of analysis and evaluation.
- --- Improve self image.
- --- Become more responsible citizens.

Students using this program are provided with a structure in which they can deal with varying points of view in a logical, orderly and rational fashion. Activities encourage students to explore and manipulate their own ideas. The student looks at his behaviors and emotions in terms of others and in view of his society and culture. By exploring the science of psychology in this way, the student can identify his behavior and their causes, develop important understandings of human behavior and explore personal thoughts and feelings.

The nature of Discovering Psychology encourages students to express ideas freely. While there are no right and wrong answers, students learn to challenge their own ideas and feelings in terms of peers and their culture. Discovering Psychology insures student success. One's own feelings and behaviors can belong only to that individual with no judgement superimposed or implied.

Discovering Psychology concentrates heavily on the area of affective development. Consistent with the Affective Domain of the Taxonomy of Educational Objectives as outlined by Krathwohl, the activities in Discovering Psychology were developed. The student gains an awareness of the world in which he lives. Acceptance of differences of race and culture and a sensitivity to human needs and problems is developed. Discussion and interaction lead to valuing. Internalization of specified values and clues to these values are explored as they are identifiable. The student looks at "attitudes" and "appreciation". Discovering Psychology is concerned with bringing together different values, resolving conflicts between them, and beginning to synthesize and internalize these concepts. By working through these activities, the student becomes better able to analyze and predict his behaviors. The students' acceptance and understanding of the needs for personal, social, and emotional adjustment are explored.

Increased skill in problem solving, self reliance techniques and cooperation with others makes Discovering Psychology a successful and desirable teaching tool.

Discovering Psychology is intended for student use and enjoyment, and is designed to help young people clarify their thinking, feelings and beliefs. The format of Discovering Psychology provides pages to be duplicated for use with students, supplemental activities for teacher selection, and suggested activities for students that do not involve written answers.

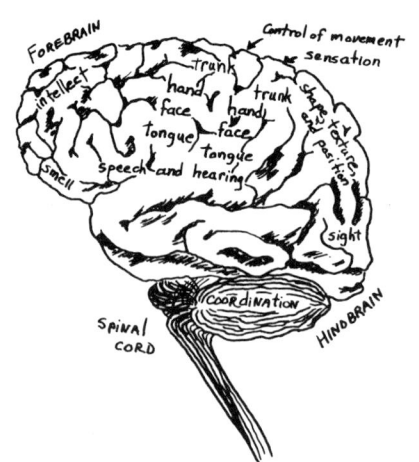

1

PSYCHOLOGY IN PERSPECTIVE

Psychology is considered to be the science of the soul and the mind. The psychologist studies man by looking at perception, learning, and problem solving. It involves the study of man and his adjustment to the world around him. It deals with man's response to stimuli, his experiences, and resultant behavior. The science of psychology considers the resultant behaviors produced by response to stimuli and experience.

This chapter will guide exploration of the science of psychology as it has developed over time. Students should build fundamental understandings to help them as the study develops. The following activities will develop necessary background information.

1. Students should be able to define and use these terms as they pertain to the study:

psychology - the science of the mind.

psychologist - scientist who studies how and why persons behave the way they do.

behavior - the ways in which people act.

mind - the organization of behavior

stimuli - something that stirs to action or causes activity.

experience - knowledge or skill gained by seeing, doing, or living through a situation.

2. Divide the students into groups to study the teachings and beliefs of Democritus, Plato, and Aristotle. Ask them to write down passages that identify the philosophers' thinking about the function of the mind. How do they compare? Make a chart to show likenesses and differences of thinking.

3. "Mind over matter" is a familiar saying. Discuss this phrase and basis in psychology. Direct students to looking at both the divisions and connections of mind and body.

4. In what is considered the modern period of the science of psychology, these philosophers had impact on the field. Research each of them. Note positions on issues related to psychology. Add them to the chart begun in Activity #2.

Descrates	David Hume	John Dewey
John Lock	E. B. Tichener	
George Berkley	G. Stanley Hall	

5. Psychology is considered to be the science of the mind. Ask five people not in your class or group to define the term mind. Compare the definitions of others found by classmates. Now look at the many definitions of the mind and compare to the definition of mind used by psychologists. After completing these activities students should be ready to complete Attachment #1. (Answers will vary.) Additional activities may be selected from these below. These additional activities can further extend the study of this chapter.

6. Discuss St. Thomas Aquinas and his theory or belief that the mind produces or results in personality. Do you agree or disagree with this idea?

7. Psychologists use a variety of instruments to measure functions of the mind. Talk with your school psychologist to learn of some of these measures of human behavior.

8. Psychologists often work with animals rather than humans, then transfer finds to human behavior

science. Can you think of reasons why animals might be used for such studies? How can results of animal studies be applied to learning about humans?

9. The study of psychology often involves one or more of the following research types: case history, survey, experimental, naturalistic observation, direct observation, and interviews. Choose one or more of these research types to learn more about. Discover what is mean by the type. How is it actually carried out?

10. Using one of the above research types, structure a study of your own that might reveal some information pertinent to the science of psychology.

11. Study the physiology of the brain. Draw a diagram to show how we believe the human brain functions. How does the physiology of the brain itself influence psychology?

12. Much research has been done on the hemispheres of the brain and their functions. Research this topic. What are characteristic functions of the right side of the brain? The left side?

Students now may wish to complete Attachment #2.

Attachment 1

PSYCHOLOGY IN PERSPECTIVE

In order to begin your study of the science of psychology, it will be necessary for you to become familiar with the term itself.

1. Use a dictionary to write a concise definition of the term psychology.

   _____
   _____
   _____
   _____
   _____

2. Now, with the aid of an encyclopedia try to expand the definition. Read introductory material in an encyclopedia. Make notes below to show what you believe to be important areas or concepts in the study of psychology.

   _____
   _____
   _____
   _____
   _____

3. Using the dictionary definition and the information you gathered from the encyclopedia, write a paragraph to describe and define the science of psychology.

   _____
   _____
   _____
   _____

Attachment 2

PSYCHOLOGY IN PERSPECTIVE

1. Are you left brained or right brained? This is a question you will be hearing more and more about. Research the topic. Then look at the list below. Put an "R" in front of activities conducted in the right hemisphere of the brain and an "L" in front of those occupying the left hemisphere.

   _____ a. thinking up a new story idea
   _____ b. memorizing a poem
   _____ c. daydreaming
   _____ d. knowing sight words
   _____ e. copying sentence from chalkboard
   _____ f. creating an idea in your mind
   _____ g. responding to emotion or feeling
   _____ h. working a long division problem
   _____ i. making a cartoon
   _____ j. using metaphors and analogies
   _____ k. writing a gramatically correct sentence
   _____ l. appreciating a musical composition
   _____ m. writing a fiction story
   _____ n. outlining
   _____ o. working an algebra problem

2. Judging from the behaviors described above, would you consider yourself to be right brained or a left brained person? Explain your answer.

   _____
   _____
   _____
   _____
   _____
   _____
   _____
   _____

2
CHARACTERISTICS OF BEHAVIOR

Students will begin to look at their behavior in relation to those of parents and siblings. Through a variety of activities students will be asked to explore the influence of heredity as compared to environment. No judgement need be imposed.

Developmental Activities

1. Vocabulary to be developed:

inherit - to receive from one's parents or ancestors through heredity.

ancestor - person from whom one is descended.

environment - the external forces, conditions, and influences that surround a being's life and affect its activities.

characteristics - a distinguishing feature or quality of a person.

heredity - all of the characteristics transmitted from parent to child.

culture - the way people learn to live in an environment.

trait - a pattern or dimension of behavior.

2. Discuss influences of environment on behavior. Show how special behavior may be appropriate in one

place, but not in others. Consider particular behaviors that might be considered acceptable by some cultures, but not others.

3. Find pictures reflective of the current culture. Make a chart with the pictures on one side and write any behaviors they foster on the other. For example, the telephone fosters closer communication over distances.

4. Project how changes in the culture might affect behaviors. Consider how your environment might be in the year 2025. Draw pictures to show the environmental changes. Now show what cultural behaviors would change as a result of these environmental changes. What adaptations would be necessary?

5. What human behaviors are alike regardless of culture? Give examples of behavior in other cultures and in yours that show likeness in humans regardless of location and condition.

6. What kinds of traits are inherited? Make a list of these (physical) traits. Choose one particular inherited trait and survey your class to determine frequency. For example, you might check to see what percentage of classmates are right handed. Now survey the parents of the same population for the same characteristic. Compare results. What generalizations can you make about your data?

7. Compare physical traits like eye and hair color, build, skin color, hair textures and others to those of your parents. Show likenesses you find. Can you find a dominance? Is there one parent you have more characteristics of than the other?

8. Identify three friends. Make a list of the cultural traits of each. Compare for likenesses and differences. Can you explain the patterns that you discover?

After discussion of both environmental and hereditary influences, students should complete Attachments #3-5. Further extension of the concept of behaviors can be attained with the following research activities.

9. Conduct a poll of classmates to determine cultural patterns in your community. You might ask questions such as "Do any of your grandparents live with you?" "Do you live in the same town as your grandparents?" "Do your parents both live with you?" "Do both parents work?" etc. The poll questions should be carefully decided and reviewed by your teacher. Select your polling sample. Graph results. Make generalizations about the cultural sample from your poll.

10. Choose a particular book character that you like and identify with yourself. Compare the book character to you and your characteristics. Consider both physical and behavioral characteristics. Make a chart to show commonalities and uniquenesses. At the bottom of the chart write a few sentences to explain why you selected the character that you did.

11. Survey your school community to determine data related to physical traits. You may wish to start with height, weight, color of hair, color of eyes, etc. Collect the data. Prepare graphs and charts to summarize the data. Make generalizations from what you have learned.

Students may further personalize the knowledge of behaviors by completing these self-reflective activities.

12. Some studies have been done by psychiatrists to indicate that people can have multiple personalities. The movies and books Sybil and The Three Faces of Eve were examples. Consider your own behavior. Do you ever feel that you act like different people? Make a list of examples. Now write a story about these seeming personality changes. You might call it The Many Faces of Me.

13. How does the community in which you live influence your behavior? Who are the important influences in your life? What activities are important to you? Does where you live have an effect on your actions and behavior? Explain by giving examples. In what instances might behaviors be different if you lived elsewhere?

Attachment 3

Behaviors

Human behavior is part of the study of psychology. In order to gain a better understanding of behaviors you will want to become an observer.

1. Watch your parent's mannerisms, those of your teacher, and those of your best friend for a period of time. Which mannerisms seem to be part of their personalities? Which are often repeated and regular? Record observed mannerisms in the chart below.

Parent	Parent	Teacher	Friend

2. Now study your own repeated behaviors or mannerisms. Put a star by any of those above that are also part of your behavior. Do you see any patterns? Whose mannerisms are most similar to yours? _____ Whose are least similar? _____
Can you think of reasons that this might be true? _____

3. Some people say, "You're just like _____" comparing us to someone else in the family. Perhaps someone has said that to you. To whom are you compared in your family? _____
Can you think of reasons that you may seem to behave in a similar way? _____

Attachment 4

Behaviors

1. Consider the meaning of environment. With that in mind list five things that you find in your classroom or school environment that are not in your regular home environment.

   _____

   _____

   _____

   _____

2. Does the presence of these items alter or change your behavior in any way? In other words, do your school surroundings cause you to behave differently that you regularly do at home? Explain your answer by giving examples.

   _____

   _____

   _____

   _____

3. Can you think of other environments that you find yourself in from time to time? Consider the house of a friend or relative, church, ball park, etc. Name at least two environments you are frequently in other than school or home. Tell what special behaviors you have in each of these environments that is different from home or school.

   a. _____

   _____

   _____

   b. _____

   _____

Attachment 5

Characteristics of Behavior

1. Phrases which describe certain behaviors are listed below. Explain how these phrases might be used.

    a. Walking a tightrope
    b. Short fuse
    c. Bare your chest
    d. Wound up
    e. Turning blue
    f. Red in the face
    g. Chicken with his head cut off
    h. Pounding your head against a wall
    i. On pins and needles
    j. Boxed in
    h. Marching to the beat of a different drum

2. Abnormal psychology deals with behaviors which are not considered normal. A person who is standing on the Golden Gate Bridge ready to jump is obviously exhibiting abnormal behavior. But what about other behaviors that are less obvious and then erupt. Read accounts in magazines, books or newspapers. Detail, in writing, abnormal behaviors exhibited.

3. Animals are sometimes used to describe people and their behaviors. Explain the meanings of these phrases and relate any phrase which has applied to you. Tell about the incident.

    a. Bull in a china shop
    b. Mad as a wet hen
    c. Clumsy as an ox
    d. Bee in his bonnet
    e. Sly as a fox
    f. Crazy as a hoot owl
    g. Slippery as an eel
    h. Crazy as a loon
    i. Water off a duck's back
    j. Fish out of water
    k. Cat out of the bag
    l. Busy as a beaver
    m. Happy as a lark

The phrase(s) related to me: _____

Attachment 5 (cont'd.)

Characteristics of Behavior

4. Animal instincts are inherent to their survival; such as squirrels collecting nuts, bears hibernating, etc. People have certain instincts too. Think about what behaviors you exhibit which you consider to be instinctive.

5. Abnormal behaviors may or may not be harmful to others. Complete a chart placing the following examples in either the normal or abnormal column. As a class, discuss your decisions. Be prepared to defend your answers.

   a. A dog mewing
   b. A 12 year old thumb sucker
   c. A two year old reader
   d. A screaming 50 year old lady
   e. An anorectia (malnutrition syndrome)

   And other questionable behaviors you can think of.

Normal	Abnormal

6. Interview twins or triplets. Conduct the interviews totally separate from each other. Ask the same questions. Chart your results as to likenesses and differences.

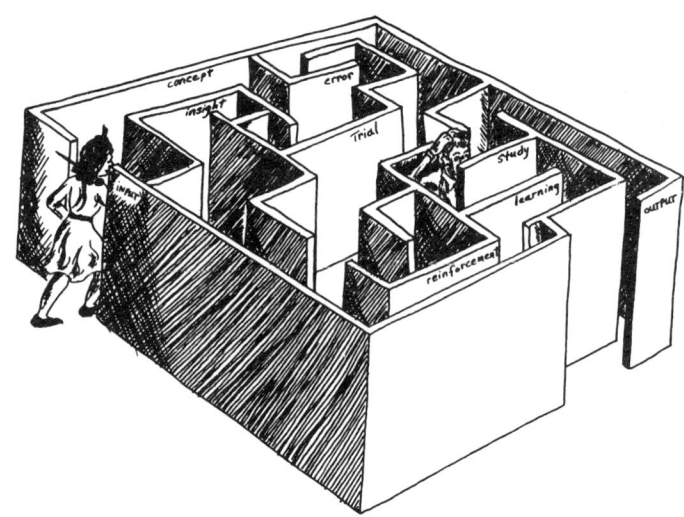

3

LEARNING

Learning is sometimes defined as changes in behavior as a result of some stimulus or change. Some things we do are inborn or inherited, but much of our behavior is learned behavior. When learning takes place behavior changes.

1. Define these vocabulary words:

   conditioning - a habitual response to a particular stimuli; usually involves reward or punishment.

   concept - building upon what you know.

   learning - modification of behavior through experience.

   insight - ability to see how the parts fit together to make the whole.

   trial and error - method of arriving at a desired result by repeated experiments or practices.

   reinforcement - a response that strengthens or reinforces learning. It may be positive or negative in type.

2. Name one thing you learned or did for the first time in the last few weeks. How did you learn about it? Who was your teacher? Why did you feel it was important or necessary to learn?

3. Make a class learning chart. Show the skill or activity learned, the source or "teacher" and the way in which it was mastered. For example:

Skill	Teacher	Method of Learning
riding a bicycle	Grandfather	Practices

4. Suppose you did not go to school at all. How would you learn then? What kinds of things might you learn? Would your curriculum be different than it is now?

Explain_____

_____

5. Conditioning is another method of learning. Rats in a maze is a traditional way to condition. Discuss other types of conditioned learning.

6. Trial and error is another way of learning. What skills have you learned by trial and error? Make a list. Do you feel it was necessary to learn these skills by trial and error? Would any other method of learning have been better?

7. Insight learning is one theory. With the definition in mind, think of something you believe you learned by insight. Explain:

_____

_____

Students should now be prepared to complete Attachments #6-10. Activities that follow provide additional experiences and extension (activities 8-10).

8. Babies learn their names through stimulus response behavior. Mother says baby's name, looks at the baby, repeats the stimulus. Baby soon learns to respond at the sound of the name. Can you give other examples of stimulus-response learning?

9. Establish a conditioned learning experiment in the classroom. Decide upon a small animal or fish for your study. What behavior will you try to teach? What stimulus will you use? How will you know conditioning has been successful or unsuccessful? Keep accurate data on your experiment. Do not set up the experiment to harm the animal.

10. Try your hand with a labyrinth. Score your attempt each time. Over a period of a week or more graph your scores. Does repeated trial reduce your error and increase your score?

11. If you have a pet, try to teach a new behavior or correct an old undesirable one by using the theory of operant conditioning.

12. Investigate programmed learning materials. Are there any such materials in your classroom or school? If so, in what ways are they used? If programmed materials are used, discuss their effectiveness with teachers and students involved.

13. Imagine that schools of the future do not have teachers, but instead have programmed materials and teaching machines. Tell what the school might be like. How would the classroom look? What are the advantages and disadvantages of this type of operant conditioning?

14. Make a list of reinforcements used by others as they interact with you during the day. Classify each reinforcer as positive (+) or negative (-). Which was most frequently used?

15. Beginning with a new born baby and taking your life to the present time, dramatize as many learning situations as you can. Use a small group for your drama. Be sure to point out the individuals who have contributed to your learning situations.

16. Read about Skinner's experiments with stimulus and response. Dramatize an experiment showing this procedure. Have your audience make conclusions.

Attachment 6

Learning

1. Conditioning is one way of learning how to behave in a given circumstance. Consider the stimulus below. What behavior does it elicit as a response?

    a. telephone rings
    b. door bell sounds
    c mother calls
    d. principal calls you
    e. favorite food cooking
    f. police siren sounds
    g. dog barks
    h. smoke alarm goes off
    i. tires screech
    j. commerical on TV

2. When behavior is rewarded, it is learned more easily. If you wanted to change your pet's behavior, how could you reward him?

    _____
    _____

3. Consider your own learning. What kinds of rewards do you receive from learning. Consider rewards by parents, teachers, peers, and others. List the rewards you get from learning. Put stars by those you feel work best.

    _____
    _____
    _____

Attachment 7

Learning

As learning progresses, you build one idea on another. This is known as building concepts. Sometimes we learn different things at different times and finally all of the information comes together in your mind. For example, when you were a baby, you probably knew very little about a dog. Now you know quite a lot.

1. Make a list of concepts you think of when you think of a dog. For example: "All dogs have four legs." Make your list as long as possible.

   _____

   _____

   _____

2. Now, draw a picture of the dog you conceptualized.

3. Compare your "dog" with others of your classmates. Compare also your list of concepts. What likenesses and differences did you see?

Attachment 8

Learning

Select a pet, a peer, or a younger child that you might teach a new skill. This is your subject. Plan carefully how you might go about teaching the skill. Consider ways that you can change behavior.

1. Write the name of your subject here: _____

2. What is your "teaching" plan? _____
   _____
   _____

3. Record your data in the spaces below. Record each attempt and the results.

Date	Attempt	Results

4. How do you judge success in learning? Look at the results of your experiment. Would you consider this teaching successful?

   Explain: _____
   _____
   _____

Attachment 9

Learning

1. Consider the various learning theories, study this list of behaviors below. Which method of learning would you think most likely? Indicate by writing beside the behavior one of these theories: conditioning, insight, trial and error.

   a. typing _____
   b. unlocking a door _____
   c. eating with a fork _____
   d. speaking _____
   e. riding a bike _____

   f. reading _____
   g. loving _____
   h. your name _____
   i. skating _____
   j. watching IV _____

2. Make a list of behaviors you have learned considering each style or theory of learning. Some will fall in several categories. Try to place them where they best fit.

Conditioning	Trial and Error	Insight
a.	a.	a.
b.	b.	b.
c.	c.	c.
d.	d.	d.
e.	e.	e.

Attachment 10

Learning

1. Behavior modifications have been used to affect learning environment. For example: tokens have been offered for "good behavior" and students may use tokens for free periods of reading, games, etc. How do you feel about rewarding people for "good behavior"? Think about a specific age group. What form might be used to modify or change behaviors which are causing learning problems?

2. Set up a stimulus-response experiment. This might be used with mice, hamsters, or other pets. Decide upon a respnse which you want such as an interest in food, responding to a sound, etc. Think of various stimuli. Experiment. Discover which one produces the quickest response. Keep a journal of your findings. Write your conclusions.

3. Is the mind ever tuned out to learning? Can you describe a situation when you felt nothing was taking place in your brain? Likewise, can you describe situations which induce the most brain activity on your part? Give examples.

4

MOTIVATION

Psychologists refer to motivation as the factor that regulates an individual's behavior in relation to his needs. Motivation fosters more effective learning outcomes. The most effective motivation for learning comes when the student sees the learning as a means to an end, regardless of what that end might be. These developmental activities will help to build necessary background.

1. Develop vocabulary for this unit.

   motivate - the thought or feeling that makes one act.

   motivation - regulation of behavior by needs.

   influence - the power of acting on others to cause change.

   internal - on the inside; inside the body.

   external - on the outside; from without.

   biological - connected with life processes; passed through heredity from parent to offspring.

2. Discuss things that influence behavior. What are the influences that are dealt with in daily life?

3. Both internal forces and external forces motivate individuals to action. Internal motivators are those like hunger and thirst. An external force might be what

others think. Make a class chart to show internal and external forces that influence or motivate behavior. Study the list carefully. Which do you think carry more weight? Explain. Which of these motives are learned? Which are biological?

4. For many people, grades are a motive for learning. Discuss grades or evaluations and marks in your school. Do you think grades influence the behaviors of students? Give reasons to support your answers. What would happen if schools stopped giving grades? Survey students to determine their reactions. Can you determine other rewards that might motivate learning and produce better results than grades? Justify.

5. Avoidance is another motivator. Can you think of behaviors you have had that were motivated by the need to avoid a consequence? What consequences help motivate you and your classmates to change your behavior in order to avoid them? Would you consider avoidance to be a strong motivational force?

Students should now be able to complete Attachments #11 and 12. Other activities to extend the study may be selected from these choices.

6. Motivation stimulates or causes behavior in others. Study a classmate for a period of time. Note any observable behaviors. What do you think may have motivated each behavior? Discuss noted behaviors with the subject. Try to clarify the motivating factors. Make a chart to show behavior, your guess, and the subject's judgement as to motivation. How do your predictions compare?

Behavior	Predicted Motive	Student's Response

7. Goal directedness and goal setting are self-motivational. Discuss goals each individual in the group has. Consider both short and long term goals. What other factors make these goals important to each individual? What other motivating factors are involved?

8. Fear and anxiety also influence behavior. List situations in which these emotions can alter or change behavior. Can you think of many behaviors where fear has been a factor? Would you say that fear plays a large or small part in influencing your behaviors? Explain.

9. Competition sometimes motivates people. Can you think of times when this is true? How do we use competition as a motivating force? Has competition ever motivated you to try especially hard at something or "go the extra mile" to achieve a goal? Give examples.

10. Consider youngsters in other cultures. Could you identify any cultures in which primary motivation is different from your own culture? How do you explain these differences?

11. You are being forced to leave the planet Earth. Leaders tell you that the group will relocate and colonize on another planet with characteristics similar to Earth. The group may take three items to facilitate the relocation. As a group you must decide on the three most important items to be taken. Because of limited space on the spacecraft, no item can be larger than the largest group member, both in height and weight. What are the motivating factors involved in your decisions?

Creative Problem Solving skills should be incorporated in this study where possible. Using the following information, set the scene for use of problem solving techniques.

12. A spaceship is leaving. The destination is the moon which, of course, has remained virtually unexplored. The passengers will be colonists in a new society. There is one space left on board the spaceship. You want very badly to go. Convince the captain that you should be included. Point out the valuable contributions you can

make in this new settlement. You may want to act this out as a drama or write your statement in the form of a position statement. Explain a drama in terms of what motivates your choices.

13. You are a teacher with a class of 20 unruly students who exhibit boredom, apathy, and do not accept responsibility for their behavior. What is the problem? What actions can you take to alleviate the problem and motivate your students?

Through role playing and drama, students can gain further understanding. These activities provide drama related experience.

14. Coaches are well known for their motivational speeches. In a group, determine a sport, the team, and a coach. Have the coach make a speech to spur the team to victory. Which coach do you feel made the best speech? Why?

Attachment 11

MOTIVATION

1. People are motivated to achieve for personal reasons. What one goal do you presently have? What motivations do you have to achieve this goal?

2. Survival itself can be a form of motivation. Find an article or story which deals with people being motivated to survive. Summarize the incidences which point out the survival instincts. (This might be better for Behavior Chapter.)

3. Stimulus - response are two terms used in the field of learning. Think about the teacher who has been able to motivate you to do your best. How was this person able to get you to perform? List as many stimuli as you can remember.

4. Think in opposite terms. What actions by teachers or others have caused negative responses from you?

Attachment 12

Motivation

1. "The devil made me do it!" For a time this was a popular response for misbehavior. Considering your study of motivation, how do you react to this explanation?
    _____
    _____
    _____
    _____

2. What control is really implied by the phrase "The devil made me do it!"?
    _____
    _____
    _____
    _____

3. Is the idea of human conscience related to this expression? Does your conscience ever exercise control over your actions?
    _____

    Can you give an example of a particular behavior that was influenced by your conscience?
    _____
    _____
    _____
    _____

4. Think for a time when your behavior might have been explained by the phrase "The devil made me do it!" Tell about the incident. Write your experience in the form of a short story with a good beginning, middle and end.
    _____
    _____

5

EMOTIONS

Emotions are feelings and reactions every individual experiences from time of infancy throughout life.

1. Define these vocabulary words:

   adrenaline - a hormone secreted by the adrenal gland which produces physiological changes associated with fear.

   emotion - a complex state involving cognitions, overt responses, internal changes, and motivation.

   mood - a mild emotional state that lingers for some time after the stimulus.

   optimism - a positive view of life.

   pessimism - a negative view of life.

   adjustment - any form of behavior that helps one adapt to the environment.

2. Brainstorm with classmates all the different emotions you can think of. Start an "emotions" chart. Whenever anyone thinks of a different emotion, add it to the list.

3. Sometimes our feelings cause physical reactions. Can you remember a time when you got "butterflies" in your stomach because you were apprehensive? Or a time

when you blushed and everyone knew that you were embarrassed? Make a list of other physical reactions that feelings and emotions cause you or others to show. List your own first, then discuss the topic with others. See how many physical signs of emotion you can list.

4. Consider your mood changes. Make a list of all the emotions you can clearly recall feeling. Use old magazines to find pictures of people showing various emotions. Make a bulletin board of collage called moods. Write a reflective essay on your mood changes.

5. Emotions and moods play a large part in our way of life. Consider people you know who are optimistic and those who are pessimistic. How are their moods different? How would you describe their emotional situation? How do their moods affect those around them?

Now students should be ready to complete Attachments 13 and 15. Other extension and enrichment activities follow.

6. You have been asked to compile a very special record album. Your task is to select songs that have special meaning to you at this time. Arrange the songs in a pleasing way and tape them. The order of the cuts may be significant to you as well. Design a record album cover. Make it reflect your own feelings and ideas.

7. Poetry is one way that we can express our feelings about the world around us. Read a wide variety of poems. Try to determine the author's feelings at the time. Choose an important time in your life or a place that has special significance for you. Write a poem that reflects your feelings.

8. Study the functions of the hypothalmus gland. How does this gland relate to and correspond with emotions?

9. What is the most frustrating experience you have ever had in your life? How did you react? This reaction was your adjustment. Make a class list of frustrations and adjustments. Can you draw any conclusions from the list?

10. Consider jobs that demand a lot of emotion or emotional stress. Make a collage of stressful jobs. Be able to tell why each should be included in the collage.

Through role playing and drama, students can gain further understanding. These activities provide drama related experience.

11. Pantomime is the art of acting without words. Using facial expressions and body actions, express the following: shock, fear, sadness, unhappiness, surprise, confusion.

12. Crying is said to be good for the soul. Prepare a skit which includes a situation for crying. Who wins the Oscar for the best "crying" scene?

Creative problem solving skills should be incorporated in this study where possible. Using the following information, set the scene for use of problem solving techniques.

13. In a small group, decide what should be done with this situation:

> You have found an elderly person who has become disoriented in the local shopping center. What steps would you take to help in this situation? After you finish, you might want to enact this to show your solutions and suggestions.

Attachment 13

Emotions

Moods and feelings are all part of emotions.

1. Use moods and feelings to make comparisons. For example, you might begin with:

    a. as mad as (a wet hen)

    b. as lonely as

    c. as sad as

    d. as happy as

    e. as depressing as

    f. as triumphant as

    g. as delightful as

    h. as excited as

Now make some more of your own

_____
_____
_____
_____
_____
_____
_____
_____

Attachment 14

Emotions

Select one time when your emotions "got the best" of you. A situation when you were so emotionally upset or so happy that you lost control might be good. Or you might consider a time when you were frightened, embarrassed, or nervous. Write a short story about the situation. Use your best narrative skills to make your reader feel the same emotions. You may choose to add illustrations.

_____

_____

_____

Attachment 15

Emotion

1. Emotions can be characterized by "emotion" words, such as fear, anger, jealousy, sadness, happiness, etc. Use one of these or another of your choice and write a poem describing this feeling. Mount your poem on paper and illustrate with color which represents this emotion to you.

2. Respond with the first idea which comes to mind as you say the following words to yourself:

   a. fear
   b. love
   c. hate
   d. anxiety
   e. jealousy
   f. security
   g. tension
   h. hope
   i. confusion
   j. anger

3. When people are excited, or in a stressful situation, adrenalin really flows - read about the physiological function and implications of adrenalin increases due to emotion.

4. Repression is a psychological term associated with emotions. Determine its meaning. Have you ever repressed anger or fear or showing of love? How did you cover up? What were your feelings at the time? How did you feel later? Why did you feel the need to do this? Express in a written essay your responses.

5. Psychosomatic illnesses are believed related to emotion. Discover several physical problems which are believed to be psychosomatic. One example might be a severe stomach ache before a test. This might be attributed to anxiety. Another example might be severe headaches which occur after an intense argument. Have you ever experienced physical discomfort which might be related to emotion?

6 THOUGHT AND PROBLEM SOLVING

Thinking is more than just reacting to stimuli. It is the mental manipulation of symbols or ideas. Thinking is the way a person uses past experience and knowledge to face new problems and situations. Thinking cannot be observed directly, but goes on and results in certain behaviors.

To develop background for this unit complete the following activities.

1. Define these vocabulary words:

    symbol - anything that stands for something else.

    concept - meaning attached to a situation.

    deductive - reasoning from general principles in one case to a similar situation.

    indicative - reasoning from facts to solutions.

    fantasy - daydreaming or imagination.

    brainstorming - a creative thinking process demanding many ideas about the same topic.

2. Consider ways ideas can be conveyed to others without using oral language. How many different ways can you think of to convey the same basic thought? Test your ideas. Which method of transmitting ideas or concepts seems most effective?

3. As we learn or extend thinking, our vocabularies often increase. Experiment with this idea. Record the conversations of very young children, your age peers, and a group of adults. Record each for exactly the same amount of time. Now tabulate the number of different words used by each age group. Does the theory of increased vocabulary hold true?

4. Reasoning is one way of manipulating symbols to justify what we do or want to do. Think of times in which running through processes have been used to explain behavior.

5. The language of advertising is designed to induce particular images and thought patterns. Collect a variety of current advertisements. Display them on posters or bulletin boards. Study the symbols the advertiser used. How do the symbols stimulate thought?

Students should now be prepared for attachments #16 and 17.

6. Read Edgar Allen Poe's <u>The Gold Bug</u>. What examples of logical reasoning do you find?

7. Memory is a large part of learning. It serves as a storehouse of experiences. Sometimes we use "tricks" to help us remember. These tricks are mnemonic devices. Catch words, jingles, and other clues are mnemonic devices. Make a class scrapbook to show the various mnemonic devices used by you and your classmates.

Thinking and thought processes help us to explore problems and research logical solutions.

8. Select three of our persons to work with you. Your group has just been alerted to a possible nuclear disaster. You have been ordered into a designated underground shelter. Space is limited, but your basic life needs will be met. The expected time to be spent in the

shelter is 4-6 weeks. The center director tells you that your group may bring three items with you to help you pass the time. Work with your group to decide what items you would take. Everyone must agree before the items can be listed. Think over the reasoning that was involved in making these decisions.

9. Develop a problem box for the class or group. Ask classmates to identify problems that they have or dilemma that concerns them. Put all problems in a box or container. Select one for the class to discuss. Consider ways to solve or at least deal with the problem. Try to identify the cause or source of the problem. Make a list of possible solutions.

Other techniques used to "walk through" the thinking process is drama or acting out. Use logical thought to help you decide how you will react.

10. Role Playing - You are on duty at a crisis center. It is late at night and pouring rain. The telephone rings. It is a young girl's voice you hear. She is on the verge of suicide, she says, and needs someone to talk to about her problem. Chose a partner and act out the situation. Try to reverse roles and see what happens.

Through role playing and drama, students can gain further understanding. These activities provide drama related experience.

11. Historians look at life in the past and make predictions about the future based on their studies. Choose several people from our past, such as Susan B. Anthony, Martin Luther King, Jr., Eleanor Roosevelt or Harry Truman. In skits, have them return to our country and make observations about problems of today, as they see them. You might want them to compare present situations to experiences of their life time.

Attachment 16

Thought and Problem Solving

Consider what symbols create positive thoughts in the minds of others. Decide upon a particular age or interest group to direct your symbols to. Now create a super-duper advertisement to sell a brand new product to the group. Because you have created it, only you know what it is or who should use it. Try out your ideas!

Attachment 17

Thought and Problem Solving

1. Problems which people face can be dealt with in a creative manner. Being able to:

    a. decide what the problem actually is
    b. determine as many possible solutions as possible
    c. think of alternatives
    d. decide on a course of action
    e. would other problems arise
    f. acceptance of the results

    Read the following situation. React using the above stated steps.

    Situation:

    A new person has moved into your school and has been placed in your class. Your two best friends have replaced your position in the group with this new person. They called you for several weeks to enter into activities but you refused because you felt left out. The new person is very cool to you as you have been since the beginning. What do you do?

2. Life problems are often contained in our subconscious and surface through dreams. Recount a recurring dream of yours.

3. Read about dreams. Is there an interpretation which fits any of your personal dreams?

7

PERSONALITY

The science of psychology looks at personality as the persistent and enduring behaviors or behavior patterns of an individual. They recognize that each personality is unique and makes no value judgement as to good and bad. Good and bad personalities are judged by those with whom they come into contact in daily life. Understanding personality helps us to predict behavior and anticipate responses.

The following activities are planned to introduce the concept of personality.

1. Develop these vocabulary words as related to this unit.

> personality - persistent and lasting behavior patterns of an individual.
>
> ego - the self as a thinking, feeling, acting being; confidence in oneself; self image; self esteem.
>
> extroversion - preoccupation with things outside oneself.
>
> id-birth - part of the personality that is inherited and present at birth.
>
> introversion - preoccupation with one's own inner experiences.
>
> trait - a characteristic used to describe a basic personality dimension.

2. Are you the "life of the party" or a "wallflower"? What types of personalities do these phrases imply? Which is introverted? Which is extroverted? Which are you? Discuss where each member of the group considers himself in relation to the extremes defined. Make a personality line reflecting each person's opinion of himself.

3. Brainstorm all of the character traits you can think of. Consider your own and those of people you know and observe. Make a class chart of personality traits you can identify.

4. Sometimes you just <u>know</u> things about a person. Have you ever sensed that you are going to like or dislike them immediately? Recall situations in which this has happened. Reflect on the circumstances and the behaviors of the person involved. What do you think influences your "first impressions" of people? Have you ever changed your opinion after you've gotten to know the person better?

5. Write a brief autobiography focusing on the events in your life that you feel really influenced your personality. Comparing and sharing autobiographies with classmates may show common influences. What generalizations can you make about influences on the personalities of you and your classmates?

Students should now be prepared to complete Attachments #18-20. Other extension and enrichment activities may be selected to further develop the unit topic.

6. Research the idea of personality evaluations through use of ink blot tests. Remember that it is the perception or perspective of the person being evaluated that influences or colors what he sees. Experiment by making several ink blots. (Drops of ink on paper folded in half will make mirror image ink blots) Try them on a sampling of people. Ask each to tell you what he sees. Do you get the same or varied responses? Can you tell anything about the personalities of your subjects from their responses?

7. Make a personality collage. Collect pictures, words, and phrases that reflect your very own personality. Make the collage say what you are! You might display class collages and try to match the person to his collage.

8. Many "beauty pageants" and other competitions consider personality as well as physical attributes. If you were the judge in a personality contest, what would you look for? How would you judge such a contest? What criteria would you use?

9. Using a picture of children (selected by the teacher) as a starting point, each member of the group should compose a story about the picture. Try to imagine what has happened, what is happening, and what will happen in the future. Share the stories. Can you tell anything about the author's personality?

10. Use your imagination and ability to express yourself. Make a list of your personality traits that make you a unique individual. Now, share them with your classmates, but use no words. You must show these traits only in a non-verbal way. Use facial expressions, pantomime, or other suitable communication forms. How many items on your list did you successfully convey?

11. Select a magazine photo of some person you do not readily identify. (Don't use movie or television personalities, sports figures, etc.) Try to put yourself in the place of the person in the photograph. Try to decide on the person's occupation, goal in life, place of residence, family role, mood, etc. Write a paragraph to give your character identity. Perhaps you will want to develop a story with your character as the main focus.

12. Play a record of an instrumental music composition. Ask classmates to write down single word reactions or short phrases that describe their reactions. Compare and contrast responses.

13. What affect does color have on you? Plan some experimenting with the influence of color on your life. How do colors effect your emotions? Give examples.

14. Consider images and stereotypes. Think of names that suggest physical characteristics or occupations. For example: Ima Hogg, or Hugh Mann Kanonbowl. How many of your own can you create?

Through role playing and drama, students can gain further understanding. These activities provide drama related experience.

15. Do animals have distinct personlities? Act out in pantomime or with sounds a chosen animal. Try to characterize the animal's personality. Have others guess "who you are".

16. Snow White had seven little friends whose names personified their personalities: Grumpy, Dopey, etc. Write and enact your original play having characters with personality trait names.

Creative Problem Solving skills should be incorporated in this study where possible. Using the following information, set the scene for use of problem solving techniques.

17. Sometimes relatives compare children because their abilities or personalities are so similar. Your great aunt Helen, who is 80 years old, continues to confuse you and your brother. This is really irritating to you. What can you do to help her remember and realize you are two separate individual and to help her to understand your feelings without hurting hers?

Attachment 18

Personality

1. Have you ever heard the expression "It takes all kinds to make the world go around"? What do you think is meant by this statement? Explain.

2. Suppose by some magical power a great change had come about. During the night all people all over the country were given the same personality. Write a story to tell about The Day Everybody Was the Same.

Attachment 19

Personality

1. Television characters often become very real to their viewers. Miss Piggy, Walter Cronkite, and Archie Bunker have recognizable faces as well as personalities. Describe the personality traits of one of them. Use examples to prove your analysis.

2. Research the physiology of the brain. Diagram the sections and the reported functions of each.

3. A great deal of research is being done with the right and left hemispheres of the brain. Read an account. Explain what is being said. Give examples from your life which point out functions using one or the other hemisphere.

4. Have you ever heard, "You're just like your father" or "That reminds me of your old Aunt Tessie"? List your family members, including yourself. Interview various people in your family or friends who have known many of you for a long time. Can you find ancestors whose personalities are apparent in your family today?

5. Personality characteristics are written in astrological charts for people being born under a certain sign. Read the characteristics given for your personal sign or another close member of your family. Do you fit the description? How?

Attachment 20

Personality

Design a very special T-shirt. Using a plain white T-shirt plan designs, lettering, etc. to convey the real you. Create your design to represent your personality as closely as possible.

You may want to hold a T-shirt personality contest for your class. Judges could select the best representations. Another idea might be to stage a personality fashion show. Everyone would wear his/her T-shirt. The commentator can describe the personalities.

8

RELATIONSHIPS

Much of human behavior is relative to the others who enter an individual's life in some way. Any interrelationship of one or more person constitutes a social relationship. This unit will look at small and large group relationships individuals may be involved in.

To build background for this unit, students should complete the activities below.

1. Define these vocabulary words as they pertain to the study:

> peer - a person who is equal or about the same age.
>
> generation gap - name given to the differences in attitudes and values from one generation to the next.
>
> group dynamics - the interpersonal relationships that develop between group members.
>
> society - the people around us.

2. What is a peer group? Who might be considered to be your peers? What kinds of peer relationships do you have? Try to determine all of the ways in which you interact with peers. How do peers influence your behavior?

3. Parents generally have a great deal of influence over their offspring. Discuss ways in which parents are

able to influence their children. Consider the ways your parents influence you.

4. Because society changes the norm or expected, behavior sometimes changes, too. Discuss with grandparents or older people in your community ways in which behaviors of young people are different now than they were 40 or 50 years ago. What societal influences might have caused those changes?

5. Sometimes the society in general furnishes a helping group or support to the individual. Brainstorm with your classmates ways in which people you do not know well (or even strangers) have helped you in different situations. On the other hand, sometimes no one is willing to come to our defense. Make a list of examples of both types of situations.

Students should be prepared to complete Attachments #21-23. Further extension and enrichment may be developed through selection of these activities.

6. Play the game gossip. Sit in a circle with a group of others. One person whispers a messsage in the ear of the next. It is passed around the circle in this fashion. The last person repeats the message aloud and compares it with that of the sender. Do you find any changes? How do you account for such changes? Does the idea of the game gossip have any implication for society?

7. Consider these agencies developed by our society to provide help to others. Choose one to research. Find out how that agency functions in society.

Red Cross   Volunteers of America
Alcoholics Anonymous   Salvation Army
Weight Watchers

What other agencies are found in your community?

8. Do both of your parents work? If you live in a single parent family, does the parent you live with work?

What are some of the ways your family copes with the situation? What duties or responsibilities do you assume to help out? How does having both parents work outside the home alter life style? How does it effect the roles of family members?

9. Friends are important to us in all stages of life, but friends change as our lives change. Discuss friendships with your parents or other relatives. Ask them to reflect on friendships they have had and how they have changed over the years. Consider your own friendships, both past and present. Can you think of reasons that some friendships continue? Can you think of reasons that some friendships change over the years? Make a list of factors that influence friendships.

10. With inflation increasing, more and more families are finding it necessary for both parents to work outside the home. What changes do you see in your community as a result of this? What changes can you predict? Consider things you believe would improve the situation.

11. Sit in a circle with classmates or group members. Study the person to your right carefully. Draw or find a magazine picture to represent a likeable or positive trait in that person. Take turns showing and telling about the positive trait in that person. Take turns showing and telling about the positive characteristic you decided was important.

12. In order to understand each other, we must be able to communicate. Make a bulletin board or chart to show all of the ways that people can use to communicate ideas. Make your display interesting and visually appealing.

Attachment 21

Social Relationships

1. An anthropologist studies the culture of a people by observations, anecdotal records, and actually living the way of life being studied. A scientist studying life in the U.S. might describe it as fast paced. Give examples which would prove or disprove this statement.

2. Think of a custom in our country which might be misinterpreted by people of other cultures due to their backgrounds. Example: watching Ohioans roasting weiners on a stick in the bush of Africa might be perceived as cooking long brown fingers. Write a short story filled with misinterpretations about our culture as written by an anthropologist from another culture. Have fun with this one!

3. A sociogram is an instrument used by psychologists to determine personal relationships. Using your classmates, fill in the following sociogram.

    a. Who would you most like to sit next to? _____
    b. Which person do you believe is the best joke teller? _____
    c. Who would you prefer as a group leader for an important project in research? _____
    d. Who is the best for writing plays and planning skits? _____
    e. Which person's soccer team would you rather be on? _____
    f. Who in this class do you consider your best friend? _____
    g. Who can the teacher usually depend upon to behave when no teacher is around? _____
    h. What two boys and two girls would you invite to a party? _____

4. Look at your sociogram. Does one person appear more than once? Why do you think this true? What traits does this person possess that you admire?

5. To perceive is "to become aware of" through one's senses; especially through sight or hearing. In relationship with others, what you see or hear affects your perception of them or the situation. Likewise, what others hear from you or see from you affects their perception of you. Conduct an experiment. Choose 25 people whom you do not know. As you pass them, make eye contact and smile a friendly smile. How many smile back? Likewise, as you pass 25 unfamiliar people, say, "Hi" or "Hello". How many respond? What conclusions can you draw from your experiment?

Attachment 22

Social Relationships

Identify one person that has influenced you or helped you in some way. This should be an important person who has caused some change in your behavior. Reflect on your relations with that person. Write a story to tell about your contact with this individual. Show how the person influenced you and caused some behavior change.

Attachment 23

Social Relationships

Friendship is an important social relationship. Why might friends be considered important? Think about the importance of your friends to you.

1. Make a list of reasons friends are important.

2. Most of us have a "best" friend. Identify a person that you consider to be your best friend. Write a short biography of that person focusing on the qualities of the person's personality that promote your friendship.

CAREERS RELATED TO HUMAN BEHAVIOR

Careers related to the field of psychology are broad and found in many walks of life. Exposure to the wide variety of help occupations will not only serve to guide students in career explorations, but will also make students aware of those persons in the world around them.

1. Vocabulary words necessary to the unit should be developed.

> career - general course of action or progress of a person through life.
>
> occupation - one's habitual employment; business, trade or calling.
>
> counsel - advice; opinion or instruction given in directing the judgement or conduct of another.

2. These careers are ones that come to mind when we talk about "self" and "personal improvement". Can you classify them into the proper cluster? You may wish to make a chart like the one below. Can you think of other helping careers that are related to a person's self-image? Add them.

psychiatrist	social worker	school administrator
psychologist	teacher	clergyman
counselor	physician	probation officer

Health Services	Public Services	Personal Services

3. Many teenagers and young people sometimes feel alone and not very good about themselves. Survey your agemates and determine some of the feelings and problems they may have experienced. Now create a job in your school to help kids. What would the person be like? What training would they need? What special qualifications would be necessary? What would the person's duties be? How would this new job help society?

4. Most of the careers related to this unit of study are classified into clusters of Public Service, Health Service and Personal Service. Can you give reasons that this might be true?

5. Make a list of occupations that might be considered "lonely" or "isolated". Here are some to get you started: night watchman, lighthouse keeper, writer, etc. What are the advantages and disadvantages of such occupations? Would any of the occupations suit you? Explain.

6. Choose one or more careers from the list in #2 and research the career you choose thoroughly. Consider training, job description, special duties, salary, places of employment, advantages and disadvantages. Is the need for this position going to remain the same, grow, or diminish in the near future? Write a report about the career(s) you chose to investigate. Include as much information as possible that might help someone else understand the career.

Now students are ready to complete Attachment #24. Further explanatory and extension activities may be selected from these choices.

Attachment 24

Careers

Write a business letter for information about careers related to psychology. Here is one source:

American Psychological Association
1200 17th Street, N.W.
Washington, DC 20036

Differentiate the major fields in psychology. What does each deal with?

1. Abnormal Psyche -
2. Clinical Psyche -
3. Comparative Psyche -
4. Developmental Psyche -
5. Educational -
6. Industrial -
7. Learning -
8. Motivational -
9. Perception -
10. Personality -
11. Physiological -

After reading about and investigating career possitiblities from the above list, choose one area in which you are interested and write a report explaining what this job would entail. Think of professions in which you might use this psychology major.

10
AN IMAGE OF ME

This unit is designed to help students look at their own personalities. It improves a variety of activities planned to draw together the ideas presented in this study. The variety of activities provides for individuals to express themselves creatively. The following activities may be used with all students to help create an appropriate display or exhibit. (These make good open house projects.)

1. Make a positives and negatives collage. Divide a large sheet of paper into two equal parts. Using words, phrases, and pictures, represent the positive you on one side and the negative you on the other. Compare your collage of self with those of others. Do any of your positives appear as negatives for others? How about your negatives? What generalizations, if any, can you make about the group?

2. Create a newspaper or giant front page featuring the accomplishments of you and your classmates. Try to feature stories about achievements, special abilities and interests. Include everyone in your class or group.

3. Identify someone in your class or group that you do not know very well. Make a list of questions that would help you to get to know that person better. You may want to ask about brothers, sisters, hobbies, interests, etc. Now interview the person. Write a short bibliographical sketch using the information you gathered. Together with others you may want to plan a "Getting to Know You" bulletin board.

4. You may want to explore the general image of your class, group, or special program. Make a questionnaire for peers to determine what image your group projects. Look at the positives and negatives. Should any of these impressions be changed? Are any perceptions inaccurate? Plan strategies to change negative images. Give some time for this to happen, then survey again to see if any changes have occurred.

5. Totally change your image for one day. Alter your dress, speech, and mannerisms to project this new you. Who do you want us to believe you are? Keep this in mind. As the totally new you, note reactions of others to you and your altered state. How do you feel in somebody else's shoes?

Students should complete Attachment #25 to help synthesize their thinking. Further extension activities are provided to add additional enrichment.

6. Consider the images of famous people. Make a list of well known persons from different walks of life that suggest an image. Include music, television, movies, politics, etc. to get a broad picture. What kind of image does each person on your list project? Is this the image desirable for him/her? Explain.

7. What animal do you consider yourself most like? Give reasons for your choice. Draw yourself in this fashion.

8. Make a filmstrip that highlights your personality characteristics and traits. Include musical background and perhaps narrative to tell about the real you.

9. Warm fuzzies are compliments or statements that make you feel good. Cold pricklies are the opposite. Discuss warm fuzzies and cold pricklies you have given and received.

10. Play the Warm Fuzzies Game. Each person in the class or group is assigned the identify of a famous person past or present. (Rock stars, television personalities, national leaders, educators, and others should

be represented.) The name of the person is printed on a tag and pinned to the real person. Now each member of the group is given five warm fuzzies. (Students may wish to design and make actual warm fuzzies or slips of colored paper can be used.) When each person has assumed his/her identity and received the correct number of warm fuzzies, the teacher or leader directs all students to give their warm fuzzies to the person or persons they most respect and admire. (Warm fuzzies are given to the person being represented, not the real person.) Guide students to examine which identities received the most warm fuzzies from the group and which received the least. Discuss the reasons for the variation.

NOTE: Warm fuzzies are compliments and/or positives that make you react positively. Cold pricklies are those slams, smears, and jabs that invoke negative emotions.

11. Find the "average" person in your class or group. Consider height, weight, hair color, eye color, etc. Come up with the composite average for those you survey. You may want to design and make an "Average Award".

12. Consider a deeply moving personal experience in your life. Write a subjective description of the situation reflecting your emotions, mood, and reactions. Concentrate on the primary mood or feeling, but others may enter into your writing as emotions do not usually isolate themselves.

13. Create a special center or interest corner by assembling articles, objects, materials, or products that reveal a personal interest. You may want to do this when others are not around and ask them to determine the person being represented.

14. Make a personal filmstrip. Consider the ideals and values that are important to you. Represent these ideas visually on filmstrip material. Choose appropriate music and/or script to accompany your visuals. Be sure the filmstrip really represents you and your ideas.

Attachment 25

An Image of Me

Make a detailed autobiography. You will want to read several autobiographies of others first. Avoid the "I was born in ----- and the -----" style of writing. Try to make your life story interesting. Choose events to tell about that were important to you. Consider times in your life when you were under stress, extremely happy, very sad, or feeling other emotions. Include persons who have been important to you. Include photographs and/or drawings to enhance your writing. Try to divide your autobiography into chapters with appropriate titles.

11

STUDENT PAGES

To increase the usefulness of this book, a duplicate set of student activity pages is provided at the very end. You can remove these pages and still retain a complete book. With permission granted, you can detach these pages for photo copying or other means of reproduction.

Attachment 1

PSYCHOLOGY IN PERSPECTIVE

In order to begin your study of the science of psychology, it will be necessary for you to become familiar with the term itself.

1. Use a dictionary to write a concise definition of the term psychology.

   _____

   _____

   _____

   _____

   _____

2. Now, with the aid of an encyclopedia try to expand the definition. Read introductory material in an encyclopedia. Make notes below to show what you believe to be important areas or concepts in the study of psychology.

   _____

   _____

   _____

   _____

   _____

3. Using the dictionary definition and the information you gathered from the encyclopedia, write a paragraph to describe and define the science of psychology.

   _____

   _____

   _____

   _____

Attachment 2

PSYCHOLOGY IN PERSPECTIVE

1. Are you left brained or right brained? This is a question you will be hearing more and more about. Research the topic. Then look at the list below. Put an "R" in front of activities conducted in the right hemisphere of the brain and an "L" in front of those occupying the left hemisphere.

    _____ a. thinking up a new story idea
    _____ b. memorizing a poem
    _____ c. daydreaming
    _____ d. knowing sight words
    _____ e. copying sentence from chalkboard
    _____ f. creating an idea in your mind
    _____ g. responding to emotion or feeling
    _____ h. working a long division problem
    _____ i. making a cartoon
    _____ j. using metaphors and analogies
    _____ k. writing a gramatically correct sentence
    _____ l. appreciating a musical composition
    _____ m. writing a fiction story
    _____ n. outlining
    _____ o. working an algebra problem

2. Judging from the behaviors described above, would you consider yourself to be right brained or a left brained person? Explain your answer.

    _____
    _____
    _____
    _____
    _____
    _____
    _____
    _____
    _____

Attachment 3

Behaviors

Human behavior is part of the study of psychology. In order to gain a better understanding of behaviors you will want to become an observer.

1. Watch your parent's mannerisms, those of your teacher, and those of your best friend for a period of time. Which mannerisms seem to be part of their personalities? Which are often repeated and regular? Record observed mannerisms in the chart below.

Parent	Parent	Teacher	Friend

2. Now study your own repeated behaviors or mannerisms. Put a star by any of those above that are also part of your behavior. Do you see any patterns? Whose mannerisms are most similar to yours? _____ Whose are least similar? _____
Can you think of reasons that this might be true? _____
_____

3. Some people say, "You're just like _____" comparing us to someone else in the family. Perhaps someone has said that to you. To whom are you compared in your family? _____
Can you think of reasons that you may seem to behave in a similar way? _____
_____

Attachment 4

Behaviors

1. Consider the meaning of environment. With that in mind list five things that you find in your classroom or school environment that are not in your regular home environment.

   _____

   _____

   _____

   _____

2. Does the presence of these items alter or change your behavior in any way? In other words, do your school surroundings cause you to behave differently that you regularly do at home? Explain your answer by giving examples.

   _____

   _____

   _____

   _____

3. Can you think of other environments that you find yourself in from time to time? Consider the house of a friend or relative, church, ball park, etc. Name at least two environments you are frequently in other than school or home. Tell what special behaviors you have in each of these environments that is different from home or school.

   a. _____

   _____

   _____

   b. _____

   _____

Attachment 5

Characteristics of Behavior

1. Phrases which describe certain behaviors are listed below. Explain how these phrases might be used.

    a. Walking a tightrope
    b. Short fuse
    c. Bare your chest
    d. Wound up
    e. Turning blue
    f. Red in the face
    g. Chicken with his head cut off
    h. Pounding your head against a wall
    i. On pins and needles
    j. Boxed in
    h. Marching to the beat of a different drum

2. Abnormal psychology deals with behaviors which are not considered normal. A person who is standing on the Golden Gate Bridge ready to jump is obviously exhibiting abnormal behavior. But what about other behaviors that are less obvious and then erupt. Read accounts in magazines, books or newspapers. Detail, in writing, abnormal behaviors exhibited.

3. Animals are sometimes used to describe people and their behaviors. Explain the meanings of these phrases and relate any phrase which has applied to you. Tell about the incident.

    a. Bull in a china shop
    b. Mad as a wet hen
    c. Clumsy as an ox
    d. Bee in his bonnet
    e. Sly as a fox
    f. Crazy as a hoot owl
    g. Slippery as an eel
    h. Crazy as a loon
    i. Water off a duck's back
    j. Fish out of water
    k. Cat out of the bag
    l. Busy as a beaver
    m. Happy as a lark

The phrase(s) related to me: _____

_____

(cut along line)

Attachment 5 (cont'd.)

Characteristics of Behavior

4. Animal instincts are inherent to their survival; such as squirrels collecting nuts, bears hibernating, etc. People have certain instincts too. Think about what behaviors you exhibit which you consider to be instinctive.

5. Abnormal behaviors may or may not be harmful to others. Complete a chart placing the following examples in either the normal or abnormal column. As a class, discuss your decisions. Be prepared to defend your answers.

    a. A dog mewing
    b. A 12 year old thumb sucker
    c. A two year old reader
    d. A screaming 50 year old lady
    e. An anorectia (malnutrition syndrome)

    And other questionable behaviors you can think of.

Normal	Abnormal

6. Interview twins or triplets. Conduct the interviews totally separate from each other. Ask the same questions. Chart your results as to likenesses and differences.

Attachment 6

Learning

1. Conditioning is one way of learning how to behave in a given circumstance. Consider the stimulus below. What behavior does it elicit as a response?

    a. telephone rings
    b. door bell sounds
    c mother calls
    d. principal calls you
    e. favorite food cooking
    f. police siren sounds
    g. dog barks
    h. smoke alarm goes off
    i. tires screech
    j. commerical on TV

2. When behavior is rewarded, it is learned more easily. If you wanted to change your pet's behavior, how could you reward him?

    _____

    _____

3. Consider your own learning. What kinds of rewards do you receive from learning. Consider rewards by parents, teachers, peers, and others. List the rewards you get from learning. Put stars by those you feel work best.

    _____

    _____

    _____

Attachment 7

Learning

As learning progresses, you build one idea on another. This is known as building concepts. Sometimes we learn different things at different times and finally all of the information comes together in your mind. For example, when you were a baby, you probably knew very little about a dog. Now you know quite a lot.

1. Make a list of concepts you think of when you think of a dog. For example: "All dogs have four legs." Make your list as long as possible.

   _____

   _____

   _____

2. Now, draw a picture of the dog you conceptualized.

3. Compare your "dog" with others of your classmates. Compare also your list of concepts. What likenesses and differences did you see?

Attachment 8

Learning

Select a pet, a peer, or a younger child that you might teach a new skill. This is your subject. Plan carefully how you might go about teaching the skill. Consider ways that you can change behavior.

1. Write the name of your subject here: _____

2. What is your "teaching" plan? _____

   _____

   _____

3. Record your data in the spaces below. Record each attempt and the results.

Date	Attempt	Results

4. How do you judge success in learning? Look at the results of your experiment. Would you consider this teaching successful?

   Explain: _____

   _____

   _____

Attachment 9

Learning

1. Consider the various learning theories, study this list of behaviors below. Which method of learning would you think most likely? Indicate by writing beside the behavior one of these theories: conditioning, insight, trial and error.

   a. typing   _____   f. reading   _____
   b. unlocking a door _____   g. loving   _____
   c. eating with a fork _____   h. your name   _____
   d. speaking   _____   i. skating   _____
   e. riding a bike   _____   j. watching TV _____

2. Make a list of behaviors you have learned considering each style or theory of learning. Some will fall in several categories. Try to place them where they best fit.

Conditioning	Trial and Error	Insight
a.	a.	a.
b.	b.	b.
c.	c.	c.
d.	d.	d.
e.	e.	e.

Attachment 10

Learning

1. Behavior modifications have been used to affect learning environment. For example: tokens have been offered for "good behavior" and students may use tokens for free periods of reading, games, etc. How do you feel about rewarding people for "good behavior"? Think about a specific age group. What form might be used to modify or change behaviors which are causing learning problems?

2. Set up a stimulus-response experiment. This might be used with mice, hamsters, or other pets. Decide upon a respnse which you want such as an interest in food, responding to a sound, etc. Think of various stimuli. Experiment. Discover which one produces the quickest response. Keep a journal of your findings. Write your conclusions.

3. Is the mind ever tuned out to learning? Can you describe a situation when you felt nothing was taking place in your brain? Likewise, can you describe situations which induce the most brain activity on your part? Give examples.

Attachment 11

MOTIVATION

1. People are motivated to achieve for personal reasons. What one goal do you presently have? What motivations do you have to achieve this goal?

2. Survival itself can be a form of motivation. Find an article or story which deals with people being motivated to survive. Summarize the incidences which point out the survival instincts. (This might be better for Behavior Chapter.)

3. Stimulus - response are two terms used in the field of learning. Think about the teacher who has been able to motivate you to do your best. How was this person able to get you to perform? List as many stimuli as you can remember.

4. Think in opposite terms. What actions by teachers or others have caused negative responses from you?

Attachment 12

Motivation

1. "The devil made me do it!" For a time this was a popular response for misbehavior. Considering your study of motivation, how do you react to this explanation?

   _____
   _____
   _____
   _____

2. What control is really implied by the phrase "The devil made me do it!"?

   _____
   _____
   _____
   _____

3. Is the idea of human conscience related to this expression? Does your conscience ever exercise control over your actions?

   _____

   Can you give an example of a particular behavior that was influenced by your conscience?

   _____
   _____
   _____
   _____

4. Think for a time when your behavior might have been explained by the phrase "The devil made me do it!" Tell about the incident. Write your experience in the form of a short story with a good beginning, middle and end.

   _____
   _____

Attachment 13

Emotions

Moods and feelings are all part of emotions.

1. Use moods and feelings to make comparisons. For example, you might begin with:

    a. as mad as (a wet hen)

    b. as lonely as

    c. as sad as

    d. as happy as

    e. as depressing as

    f. as triumphant as

    g. as delightful as

    h. as excited as

Now make some more of your own

_____
_____
_____
_____
_____
_____
_____
_____
_____
_____

Attachment 14

Emotions

Select one time when your emotions "got the best" of you. A situation when you were so emotionally upset or so happy that you lost control might be good. Or you might consider a time when you were frightened, embarrassed, or nervous. Write a short story about the situation. Use your best narrative skills to make your reader feel the same emotions. You may choose to add illustrations.

_____

_____

_____

(cut along line)

Attachment 15

Emotion

1. Emotions can be characterized by "emotion" words, such as fear, anger, jealousy, sadness, happiness, etc. Use one of these or another of your choice and write a poem describing this feeling. Mount your poem on paper and illustrate with color which represents this emotion to you.

2. Respond with the first idea which comes to mind as you say the following words to yourself:

   a. fear
   b. love
   c. hate
   d. anxiety
   e. jealousy
   f. security
   g. tension
   h. hope
   i. confusion
   j. anger

3. When people are excited, or in a stressful situation, adrenalin really flows - read about the physiological function and implications of adrenalin increases due to emotion.

4. Repression is a psychological term associated with emotions. Determine its meaning. Have you ever repressed anger or fear or showing of love? How did you cover up? What were your feelings at the time? How did you feel later? Why did you feel the need to do this? Express in a written essay your responses.

5. Psychosomatic illnesses are believed related to emotion. Discover several physical problems which are believed to be psychosomatic. One example might be a severe stomach ache before a test. This might be attributed to anxiety. Another example might be severe headaches which occur after an intense argument. Have you ever experienced physical discomfort which might be related to emotion?

Attachment 16

Thought and Problem Solving

Consider what symbols create positive thoughts in the minds of others. Decide upon a particular age or interest group to direct your symbols to. Now create a super-duper advertisement to sell a brand new product to the group. Because you have created it, only you know what it is or who should use it. Try out your ideas!

Attachment 17

Thought and Problem Solving

1. Problems which people face can be dealt with in a creative manner. Being able to:

    a. decide what the problem actually is
    b. determine as many possible solutions as possible
    c. think of alternatives
    d. decide on a course of action
    e. would other problems arise
    f. acceptance of the results

    Read the following situation. React using the above stated steps.

    Situation:

    A new person has moved into your school and has been placed in your class. Your two best friends have replaced your position in the group with this new person. They called you for several weeks to enter into activities but you refused because you felt left out. The new person is very cool to you as you have been since the beginning. What do you do?

2. Life problems are often contained in our subconscious and surface through dreams. Recount a recurring dream of yours.

3. Read about dreams. Is there an interpretation which fits any of your personal dreams?

Attachment 18

Personality

1. Have you ever heard the expression "It takes all kinds to make the world go around"? What do you think is meant by this statement? Explain.

2. Suppose by some magical power a great change had come about. During the night all people all over the country were given the same personality. Write a story to tell about The Day Everybody Was the Same.

Attachment 19

Personality

1. Television characters often become very real to their viewers. Miss Piggy, Walter Cronkite, and Archie Bunker have recognizable faces as well as personalities. Describe the personality traits of one of them. Use examples to prove your analysis.

2. Research the physiology of the brain. Diagram the sections and the reported functions of each.

3. A great deal of research is being done with the right and left hemispheres of the brain. Read an account. Explain what is being said. Give examples from your life which point out functions using one or the other hemisphere.

4. Have you ever heard, "You're just like your father" or "That reminds me of your old Aunt Tessie"? List your family members, including yourself. Interview various people in your family or friends who have known many of you for a long time. Can you find ancestors whose personalities are apparent in your family today?

5. Personality characteristics are written in astrological charts for people being born under a certain sign. Read the characteristics given for your personal sign or another close member of your family. Do you fit the description? How?

Attachment 20

Personality

Design a very special T-shirt. Using a plain white T-shirt plan designs, lettering, etc. to convey the real you. Create your design to represent your personality as closely as possible.

You may want to hold a T-shirt personality contest for your class. Judges could select the best representations. Another idea might be to stage a personality fashion show. Everyone would wear his/her T-shirt. The commentator can describe the personalities.

Attachment 21

Social Relationships

1. An anthropologist studies the culture of a people by observations, anecdotal records, and actually living the way of life being studied. A scientist studying life in the U.S. might describe it as fast paced. Give examples which would prove or disprove this statement.

2. Think of a custom in our country which might be misinterpreted by people of other cultures due to their backgrounds. Example: watching Ohioans roasting weiners on a stick in the bush of Africa might be perceived as cooking long brown fingers. Write a short story filled with misinterpretations about our culture as written by an anthropologist from another culture. Have fun with this one!

3. A sociogram is an instrument used by psychologists to determine personal relationships. Using your classmates, fill in the following sociogram.

   a. Who would you most like to sit next to? _____
   b. Which person do you believe is the best joke teller? _____
   c. Who would you prefer as a group leader for an important project in research? _____
   d. Who is the best for writing plays and planning skits? _____
   e. Which person's soccer team would you rather be on? _____
   f. Who in this class do you consider your best friend? _____
   g. Who can the teacher usually depend upon to behave when no teacher is around? _____
   h. What two boys and two girls would you invite to a party? _____

4. Look at your sociogram. Does one person appear more than once? Why do you think this true? What traits does this person possess that you admire?

5. To perceive is "to become aware of" through one's senses; especially through sight or hearing. In relationship with others, what you see or hear affects your perception of them or the situation. Likewise, what others hear from you or see from you affects their perception of you. Conduct an experiment. Choose 25 people whom you do not know. As you pass them, make eye contact and smile a friendly smile. How many smile back? Likewise, as you pass 25 unfamiliar people, say, "Hi" or "Hello". How many respond? What conclusions can you draw from your experiment?

Attachment 22

Social Relationships

Identify one person that has influenced you or helped you in some way. This should be an important person who has caused some change in your behavior. Reflect on your relations with that person. Write a story to tell about your contact with this individual. Show how the person influenced you and caused some behavior change.

Attachment 23

Social Relationships

Friendship is an important social relationship. Why might friends be considered important? Think about the importance of your friends to you.

1. Make a list of reasons friends are important.

2. Most of us have a "best" friend. Identify a person that you consider to be your best friend. Write a short biography of that person focusing on the qualities of the person's personality that promote your friendship.

Attachment 24

Careers

Write a business letter for information about careers related to psychology. Here is one source:

>American Psychological Association
>1200 17th Street, N.W.
>Washington, DC 20036

Differentiate the major fields in psychology. What does each deal with?

1. Abnormal Psyche -
2. Clinical Psyche -
3. Comparative Psyche -
4. Developmental Psyche -
5. Educational -
6. Industrial -
7. Learning -
8. Motivational -
9. Perception -
10. Personality -
11. Physiological -

After reading about and investigating career possitiblities from the above list, choose one area in which you are interested and write a report explaining what this job would entail. Think of professions in which you might use this psychology major.

Attachment 25

An Image of Me

Make a detailed autobiography. You will want to read several autobiographies of others first. Avoid the "I was born in ----- and the -----" style of writing. Try to make your life story interesting. Choose events to tell about that were important to you. Consider times in your life when you were under stress, extremely happy, very sad, or feeling other emotions. Include persons who have been important to you. Include photographs and/or drawings to enhance your writing. Try to divide your autobiography into chapters with appropriate titles.